Anonymous

The Money Question in 1813 and 1863

what some did then, others are seeking to do now

Anonymous

The Money Question in 1813 and 1863
what some did then, others are seeking to do now

ISBN/EAN: 9783337891114

Printed in Europe, USA, Canada, Australia, Japan

Cover: Foto ©Andreas Hilbeck / pixelio.de

More available books at **www.hansebooks.com**

THE

MONEY QUESTION

IN

1813 AND 1863.

WHAT SOME DID THEN, OTHERS ARE SEEK-
ING TO DO NOW.

By A LOYAL CITIZEN.

NEW YORK:

ANSON D. F. RANDOLPH,

BOOKSELLER AND PUBLISHER,

NO. 683 BROADWAY.

1863.

THE MONEY QUESTION

IN 1814 AND 1863.

Faction, the child of unhallowed ambition and low instincts, is a cosmopolite. It is also nomadic—as migratory as tent-dwellers. It has been found in all countries and in all ages. Its character has ever been the same. It is a charlatan, yet it never lacks dupes and admirers. History is spiced with its pungent elements. Our own is full of it. It was known in the Continental Congress and in the Continental Army. It ran riot during the weak Confederacy, and was impudent and defiant to the last degree, under the name of Democracy, while Washington was Chief Magistrate of the Republic. When Jefferson became President it left Virginia, its genial seat, and for a dozen years made New England ridiculous by its follies and vices. It took possession of South Carolina more than thirty years ago, and left there a brood of vipers that have hissed horribly for a few years past. It is now planting its stations and endeavoring to gain a foothold in the loyal states, under the specious name of "Peace Party," the title by which it was known in New England and pilloried by the patriotism of the nation during the war of 1812–'15.

Then, as now, the Peace Party was hypocritical and vulgar. Then, as now, its component parts were few and often obscure, and its strength was in its impudence and bluster. Then, as now, it worshiped *party* and forsook *country*. Then, as now, it clamored loudly about the sanctity of the Constitution, while it constantly violated the dearest principles of its spirit, and sought to paralyze the arm earnestly endeavoring to preserve it and save the republic from destruction. Then (as it will now) it utterly failed, because of the viciousness of its motives. The New England "factionist" of 1814 was like the "factionist" of New York and other states in 1863, with this essential difference—he was never mean enough to abuse the cradle in which he was rocked, or kick the mother that bore him.

The Federal or opposition party during the war of 1812, was then known as the peace party, but it was only a factious few of that party who were willing to have peace on *any terms.* Leading men like Quincy, of Massachusetts, and Emott, of New York, while they deprecated the war as unnecessary, frowned indignantly upon those who were ready to embarrass the Government when engaged in a struggle with a powerful foe. The "disloyalists" of fifty years ago held the same relation to the Federal party, as the "disloyalists" of our day do to the Democratic party. The great mass of the Federal party were patriotic, the great mass of the Democratic party are patriotic. The peace-at-any-price men—then, as now, were generally second-rate politicians, hopeless of any but Ephesian fame ; possessed of more cunning than talent, utterly without moral convictions, selfish, loving *party* and their own lusts more than *country* and their fellow-men, and possessing wealth enough to purchase, directly or indirectly, the services of a few venal presses.

TACTICS OF THE PEACE MEN IN 1814.

Among others of their wicked schemes—a scheme about to be adopted by the "factious few" of to-day—for embarrassing the Government, was *an assault upon the public credit. They* sought, by that and other means, to place the destinies of their country in the hands of Great Britain. The same class of politicians now seek to place the destinies of their country in the hands of a few slaveholders by the same means. Let us consider a few facts of the past.

For several years previous to the war, and during its earlier stages, embargo acts and other measures restrictive of commerce had been adopted to compel Great Britain to be just. These acts were naturally distasteful to commercial New England, and the "peace men" of that day so inflamed a large interested class against the measures of the Government, and even the Government itself, that the navigation laws were openly defied, and magistrates would not take cognizance of their violations of them. Smuggling became so general in that region during the war, that one of the most eminent of the New England opponents of the administration was constrained to confess that a class of citizens, "encouraged," as he said, "by the just odium against the war, sneer at the restraints of conscience, laugh at perjury, mock at loyal restraints, and acquire an ill-gotten wealth at the expense of public morals and of the more sober, conscientious part of the community." He charged the administration and the war with the authorship of that "monstrous depravation of morals," that "execrable course of smuggling and fraud."

Boston was the great center of this contraband trade, a business very little engaged in south of the Connecticut river. The consequence was that foreign goods, shut out from other seaports, found their way there. Many valuable British prizes were also sent into Boston, and added greatly to the stock of foreign merchandise there. The merchants of New York, Philadelphia, and the cities further south were necessarily dependent upon Boston for a supply of such goods, for which they paid partly in bills of the banks of the Middle and Southern States, and partly in their own promissory notes. By this means Boston became a financial autocrat, having in its hands despotic power to control the money affairs of the whole country. This fact suggested to the New England faction a villainous scheme for crippling the Government and building up their party upon the ruins of a dishonored republic. They were quick to act upon the suggestion and put their scheme into operation.

DEPRECIATING THE CURRENCY IN 1814.

From the beginning of the war the Government was compelled to ask for loans. The Peace Party at political meetings, through the press, and in the pulpit, cast every possible obstacle in the way. In the spring of 1814, the darkest hour of the war, this opposition took the form of virtual treason. The Government was weak, and its internal enemies knew it; and in proportion to its exhibition of weakness they became bold and outspoken. "Will Federalists subscribe to the loan? Will they lend money to our national rulers?" a leading Boston paper significantly asked. "It is impossible, first, because of the principle, and secondly, because of *principal* and *interest*. If they lend money now, they make themselves parties to the violation of the Constitution, the cruelly oppressive measures in relation to commerce, and to all the crimes which have occurred in the field and in the cabinet. . . . Any Federalist who lends money to the Government will be called *infamous!*" The people were then adroitly warned that money loaned to the Government would not be safe. "How, where, and when," asked this disloyal newspaper, "are the Government to get money to pay interest?" Then, in language almost the same as that of a distinguished Democratic leader in this State, a threat of future *repudiation* was thrown out, to create distrust in the Government securities. "Who can tell," said the writer above alluded to, "whether *future rulers may think the debt contracted under such circumstances, and by men who lend money to help out measures which they have loudly and constantly condemned, ought to be paid.*"

Another newspaper said of the Boston merchants : "They will lend the Government money to retrace their steps, but none to persevere in their present course. Let every highwayman find his own pistols." And a Doctor of Divinity shouted from the pulpit at Byfield : "If the rich men continue to furnish money, war will continue till the mountains are melted with blood—till every field in America is white with the bones of the people ;" while another said : "Let no man who wishes to continue the war by active means, by vote or lending money, dare to prostrate himself at the altar on the Fast Day, for such are actually as much partakers in the war as the soldier who thrusts his bayonet, and the judgment of God will await them."

These extracts give but a faint idea of the violence of these men in the New England capital at that time. By inflammatory and threatening publications and personal menaces they intimidated many capitalists. These were afraid to negotiate for the loan openly, a fact which the advertisements of brokers at that time have placed on record. Gilbert & Dean advertised that the "names of all subscribers shall be known only to the undersigned." Another made it known that "the name of every applicant shall, at his request, be known only to the subscriber." Another assured the people that he had made arrangements "for perfect secrecy in the transactions of his business."

These advertisements excited the venom of the peace party exceedingly, and they poured abuse upon the subscribers and the Government together. "Money," said one of the most prominent among them, with great bitterness, "is such a drug (the surest signs of the former prosperity and present insecurity of trade) that men against their consciences, their honor, their duty, their professions and promises, are willing to lend it secretly to support the very measures which are both intended and calculated for their ruin." Another said : "How degraded must our Government be, even in her own eyes, when they resort to such tricks to obtain money, which a common Jew broker would be ashamed of. They must be well acquainted with the fabric of the men who are to loan them money, when they offer, that if they will have the goodness to do it, their names shall not be exposed to the world."

PATRIOTISM OF THE PEOPLE, AND NEW SCHEMES OF THE PEACE MEN.

But all these efforts at intimidation failed to prevent the loan. Patriotic men in New England, of the opposition school, subscribed to the loan; and in the Middle States the Federalists did so openly and liberally, to the disgust and mortification of the traitorous few. This caused them to try another and more infamous scheme, as follows:

We have observed that, for reasons named, Boston became the centre of financial power. These men determined to use that power to embarrass the Government. The banks in the Middle and Southern States were the principal subscribers to the loan, and the traitors determined to drain them of their specie, and thus produce an utter inability to pay their subscriptions. Some of the Boston banks became parties to the scheme. The notes of the banks in New York, Philadelphia, and places further south, held by their banks, were transmitted to them with demands for specie, and at the same time drafts were drawn on the New York banks for the balances due the Boston corporations, to the amount, in the course of a few months, of about eight millions of dollars. The New York bankers were compelled to draw largely on those of Philadelphia, Philadelphia bankers on those of Baltimore, and so on. A panic was created. No one could predict the result. Confidence was shaken. Wagons were seen loaded with specie leaving bank doors, with the precious freight going from city to city, to find its way finally into the vaults of those of Massachusetts. The banks, thus drained, were compelled to curtail their discounts. Commercial derangement and bankruptcies ensued. Subscribers to the loan were unable to comply with their promises, and so uncertain was the future to the minds of many who intended to subscribe, that they hesitated. When the Boston bankers were called upon by public opinion to explain their movement, they made the specious plea of their right to the balances due them from other banks. This was not satisfactory. Matthew Carey, one of the ablest publicists of the day, says that the demand was made at a season of the year when freight on the specie, on account of the bad state of the roads, was from twenty to thirty per cent. more than it would have been had they waited a few weeks. That they could have waited, without detriment to any interest, is made manifest by the following statement of the condition of the banks in Massachusetts, in January, 1814, just before the movement was made:

	Specie.		Notes in Circulation.
Massachusetts Bank,........	$2,114,164	....	$682,708
Union, ...	657,795	....	283,225
Boston, ...	1,182,572	....	369,903
State, ...	659,066	....	509,000
New England,............	284,456	....	161,170
Mechanics,..............	47,391	....	44,595
	$4,945,444	....	$2,000,601

By this statement, it appears that they had in their vaults about $250 in specie for every $100 of their notes in circulation; "a state of things," says Carey, "probably unparalleled in the history of banking, from the days of the Lombards to the present time."

The effects of the conspiracy were potent and ruinous, and for a while it was thought impossible for the Government to sustain its army and navy. The banks out of New England were compelled to suspend specie payments; and the injurious effects upon the paper currency of the country may be seen by the following price current, published on the 7th of February, 1815:

	Below Par.	
All the banks in New York State, Hudson and Orange excepted,................	19 to 20	per cent.
Hudson Bank,.........................	20	"
Orange Bank,.........................	24	"
Philadelphia City Banks,..............	24	"
Baltimore Banks,.....................	30	"
Treasury Notes, ...	24 to 25	"
United States Six per cents...........	30	"

Stocks of banks, insurance companies, and other corporations suffered great depreciation, to the injury of thousands of innocent people, such as widows and orphans. Had the conspirators fully succeeded, the national armies must have been disbanded, and the Government reduced to a dependency of Great Britain.

INTRIGUES WITH THE PUBLIC ENEMY.

To make the blow against the public credit still more effectual, the conspirators made arrangements with agents of the

Government authorities of Lower Canada, whereby a very large amount of British Government bills, drawn on Quebec, were transmitted to New York, Philadelphia, and Baltimore, and sold on such advantageous terms to capitalists, as induced them to purchase. These transactions were made so boldly that advertisements like the following appeared in the Boston papers:

1 bill for............£800	British Government Bills	
1 do. 250	for sale by	
1 do. 203	CHARLES W. GREEN,	
————	No. 14 India Wharf.	
£1,253		

By this means an immense amount of gold was transmitted to Canada, placed beyond the reach of the Government of the United States, and put into the hands of the enemy to give sinews to the war they were waging against the independence of the Republic. So great was this drain and the demand for specie to pay for smuggled goods brought from Canada and Nova Scotia, that the specie in the Massachusetts banks was reduced in the course of six months nearly three millions and a half of dollars—the amount being $5,468,604 on the 1st of July, 1814, and only $1,999,368 on the 1st of January, 1815.

REJOICINGS OF THE PEACE MEN AT THE COUNTRY'S MISFORTUNES.

From the very beginning of the war, a factious few of the opposition made such persistent onslaught upon the Government, for the purpose of embarrassing the Administration, that a bonus was paid for all sums loaned. In January, 1813, a loan of $16,000,000 was authorized It was obtained principally from individuals at the rate of $88, for a certificate of stock for $100, by which lenders received a bonus on that small loan of $2,100,377. In August, the same year, a further loan of $7,500,000 was authorized. It was taken at $113 31-100, at six per cent. In March, 1814, a loan of $25,000,000 was authorized. This was the loan which the factionists of New England so vehemently warned the people against. Only $11,400,000 of it were raised, for which certificates were given to the amount of $14,262,351, giving a bonus to lenders of that small amount of $2,852,000. These terms were so disastrous to the Government, that no more attempts were made to loan money during the war, the deficiency being made up by the issue of Treasury notes to the amount of $18,452,800.

This injury to the Government credit was gloated over by the " Peace men." One of them, writing from Boston to a New York newspaper in February, 1815, said exultingly: "This day twenty thousand dollars six per cent. stock was put up at auction, five thousand dollars of which only was sold, for want of bidders, and that at forty per cent. under par. As for the former war loan, it would be considered little short of an insult to offer it in the market, it being a very serious question who is to father the child *in case of national difficulties.*"

This last expression refers to the hopes of the conspirators, of bringing about a dissolution of the Union by means of the Hartford Convention, which had adjourned to meet again, if necessary. It is proper to add that their hopes would have been frustrated, for that Convention was too essentially patriotic in the designs of a great majority of its members to have given the vile traitors any comfort. It may also be proper to add, for the gratification of the reader and as a warning to the factionists of to-day, that many of those of 1814 suffered severely by the very distresses their villanies had produced, and that they were ever detested by all honorable men. They were consigned to everlasting social and political obscurity.

Similar enemies of the country are now, in various ways, endeavoring to alarm the people concerning the national finances. Every art which wickedness can divine will be used to accomplish their vile purpose. They expatiate largely on the fearful rise in gold. They quote the action of men of great means, who will not hold any amount of United States currency, but are investing all their surplus funds in *State* stocks, or real estate. They suggest an impending financial crisis, such as the country has never experienced. They roll up their eyes and cast up their hands in pretended horror because of the " crushing national debt." They hint darkly of repudiation by a new administration, and thus hope to destroy confidence in the public stocks, and they point malignantly to the " Continental money " now in the cabinets of the curious, as foreshadowing the fate of the Government currency, which they declare will " *never be redeemed.*" A few words on that point, and I will close.

CONTINENTAL CURRENCY.

When the continental paper currency was rapidly depreciating, and its redemption no longer a probability, the Continental Congress addressed the people on the subject, and said, in substance: "Suppose at the end of the war, the amount of unredeemed bills of credit shall be $200,000,000, and the loans $100,000,000. The National Debt would then be $300,000,000. We are a people 3,000,000 in number, making the burden on each, $100. Fund the debt, and make it payable in twenty years, and it makes $5 a year for each person. Assess men according to their estates, and how few would be called upon to pay anything! Then consider that the population will double in twenty years, making the payment proportionately easier."

Thus hopefully argued the fathers, when there was no National Government to levy a dollar of taxes, and the resources of the country were undeveloped and unsuspected. How will this reasoning apply now? Suppose our national debt, at the close of this war, shall be $3,000,000,000, or ten times that of 1783. We are now a people more than 30,000,000 in number, or ten times as many as the fathers named. The remainder of their argument will apply to our case exactly, with the extremely important fact added, that we have a National Government that bears the loyalty of the vast majority of the people, and with powers for taxation equal to any exigency that may be contemplated, while the resources of the country, developed and known, are incalculable. Looking at facts as they stand, no intelligent, *honest* man will say to his neighbor—"Don't trust the Government securities; the 'greenbacks' will never be redeemed." He *knows* better. Be assured that every man of that stamp is of the "copperhead persuasion," and loves party more than the *republic*.